THIS BOOK

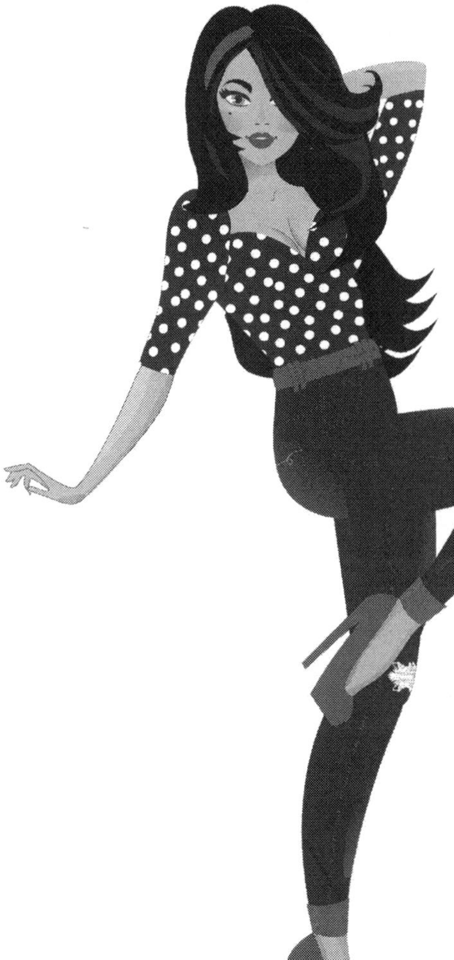

BELONGS TO:

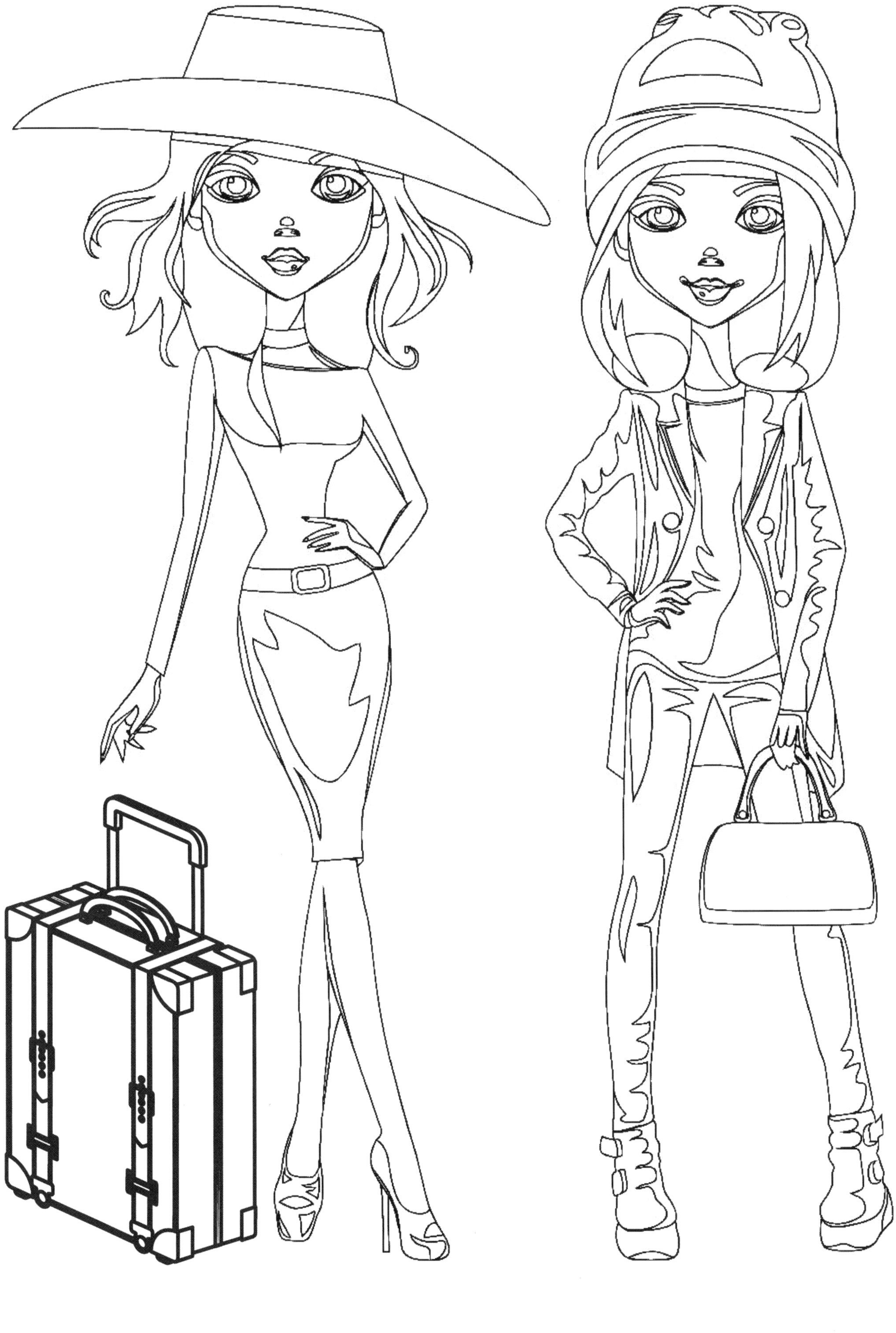

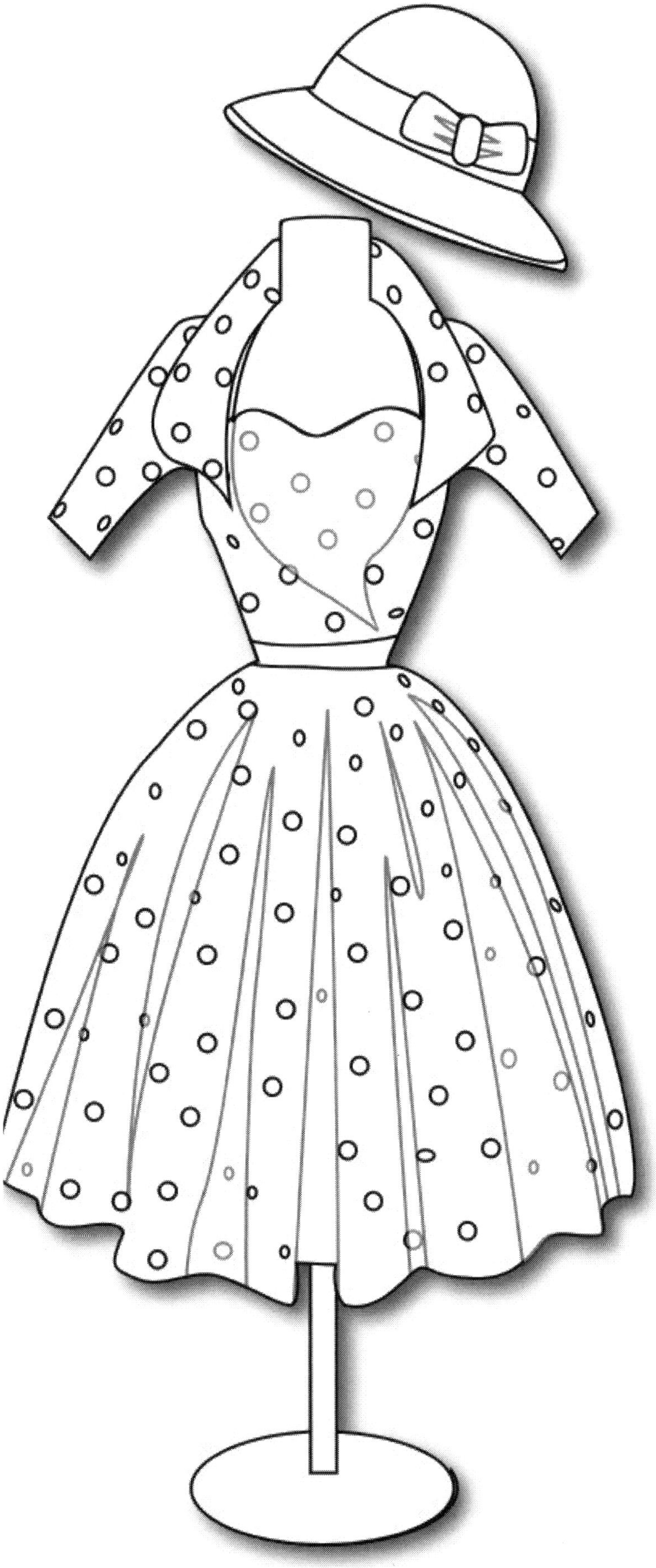

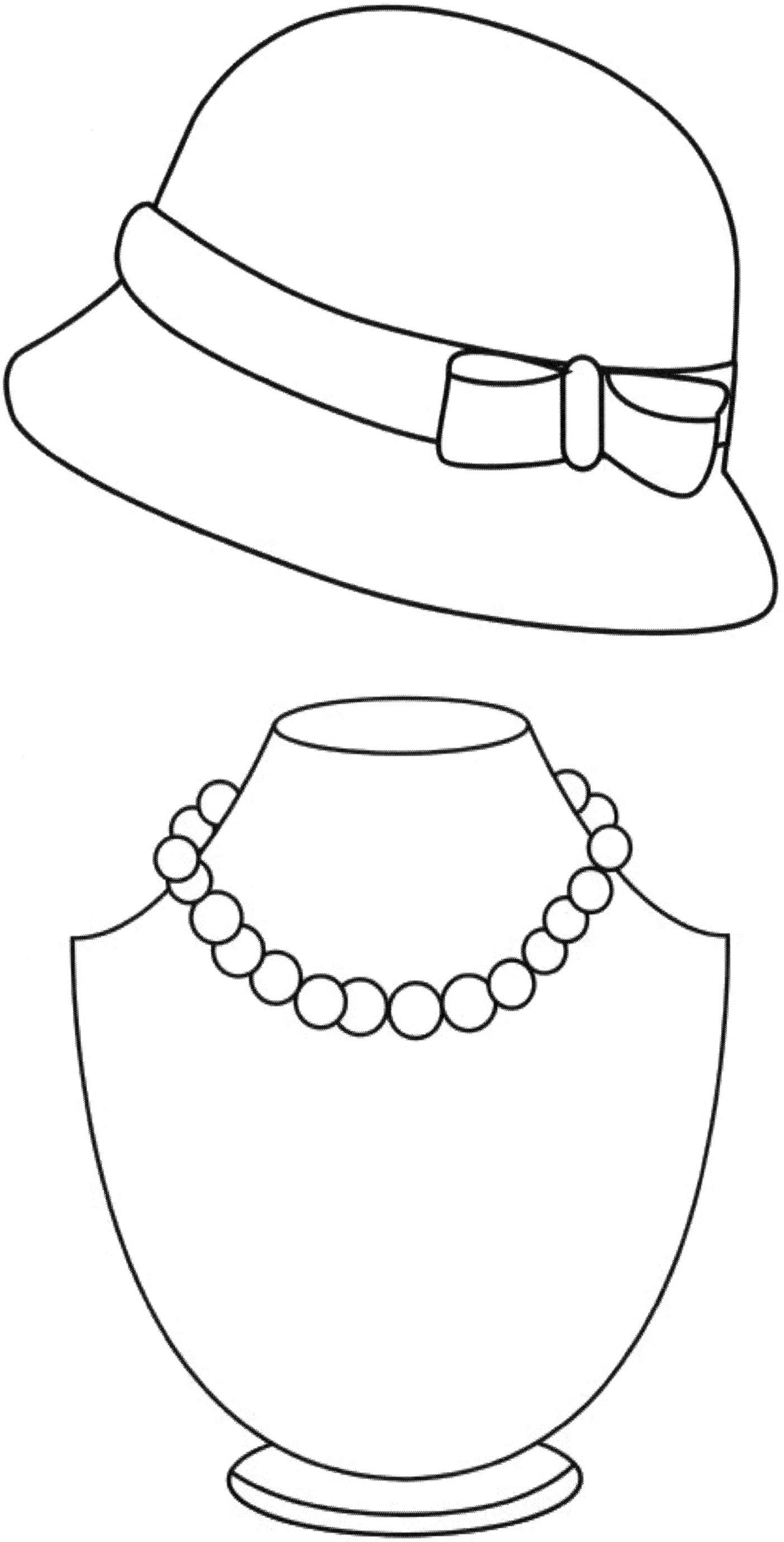

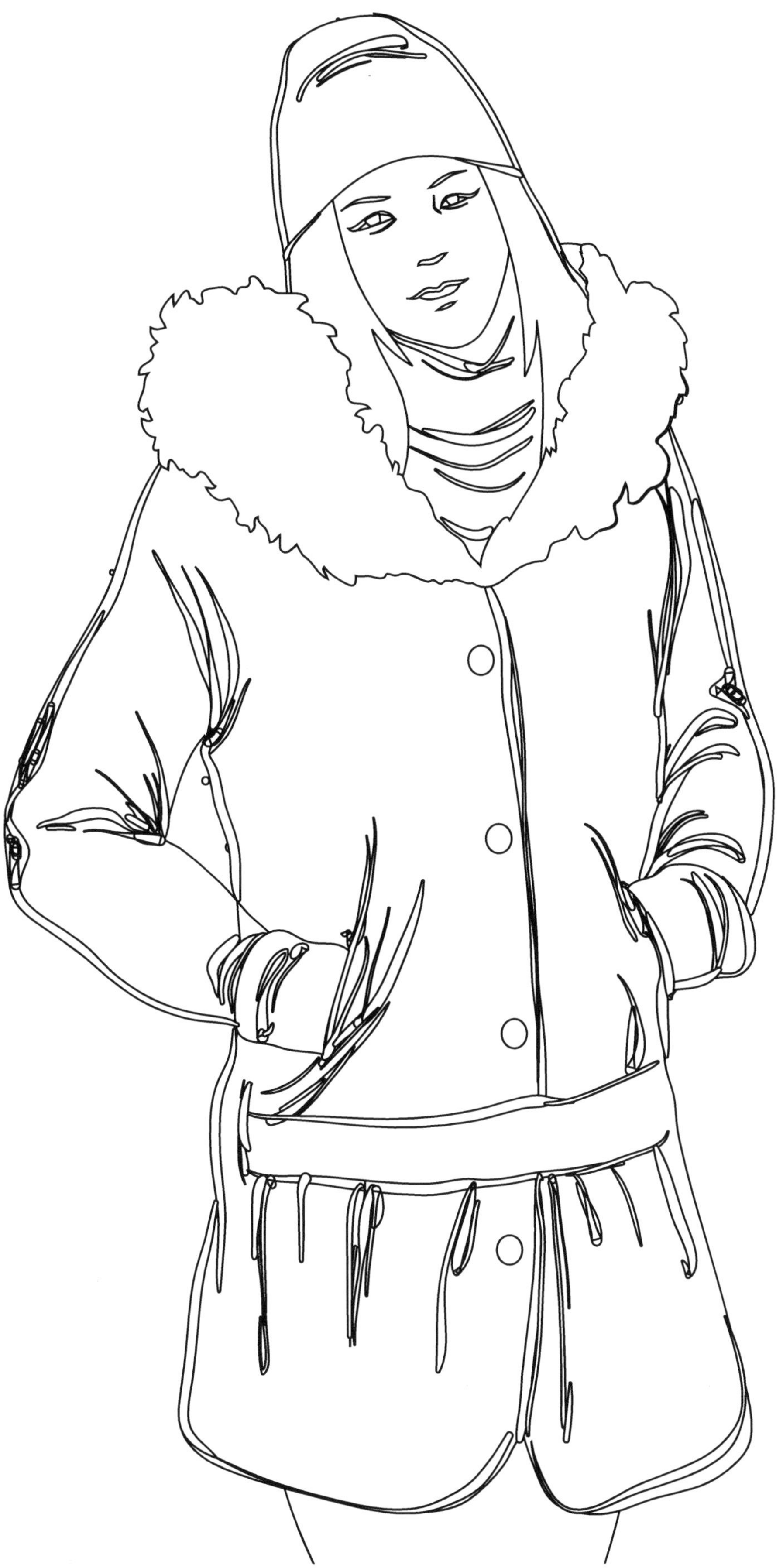

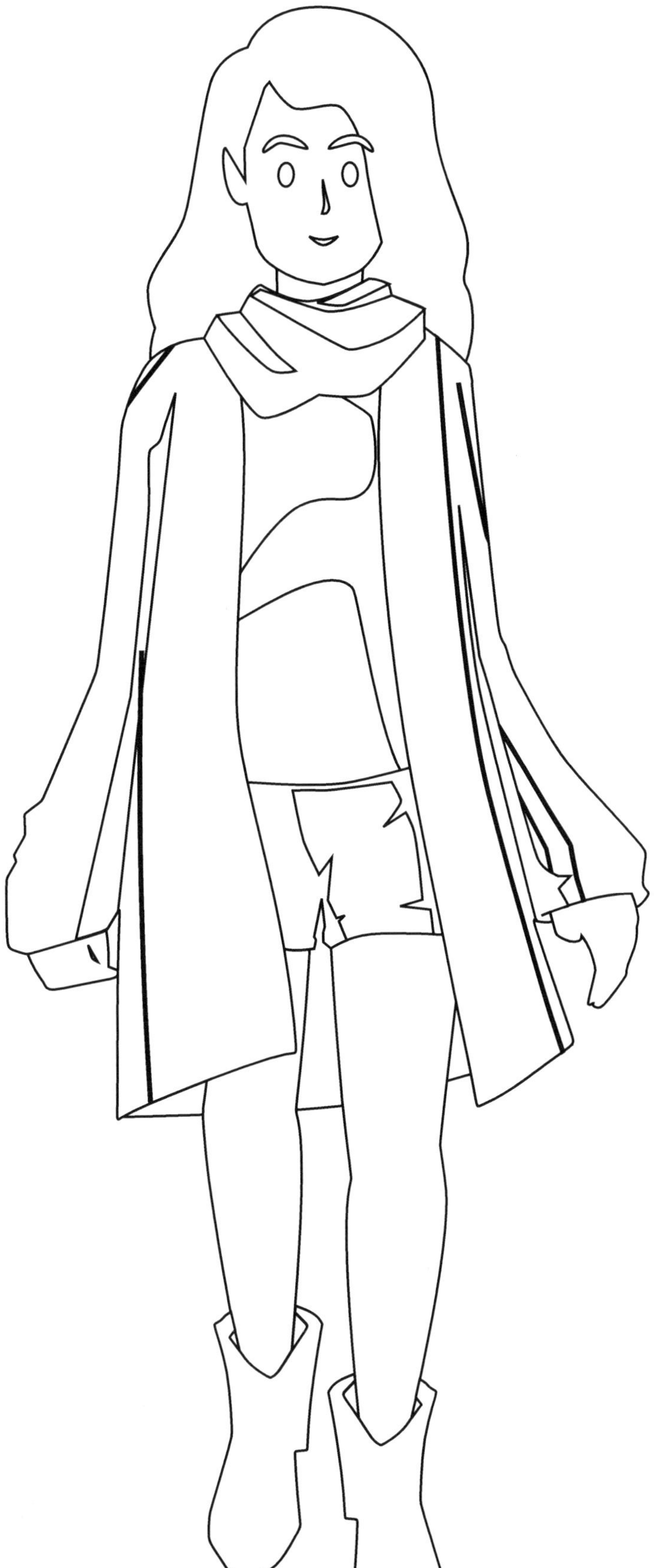

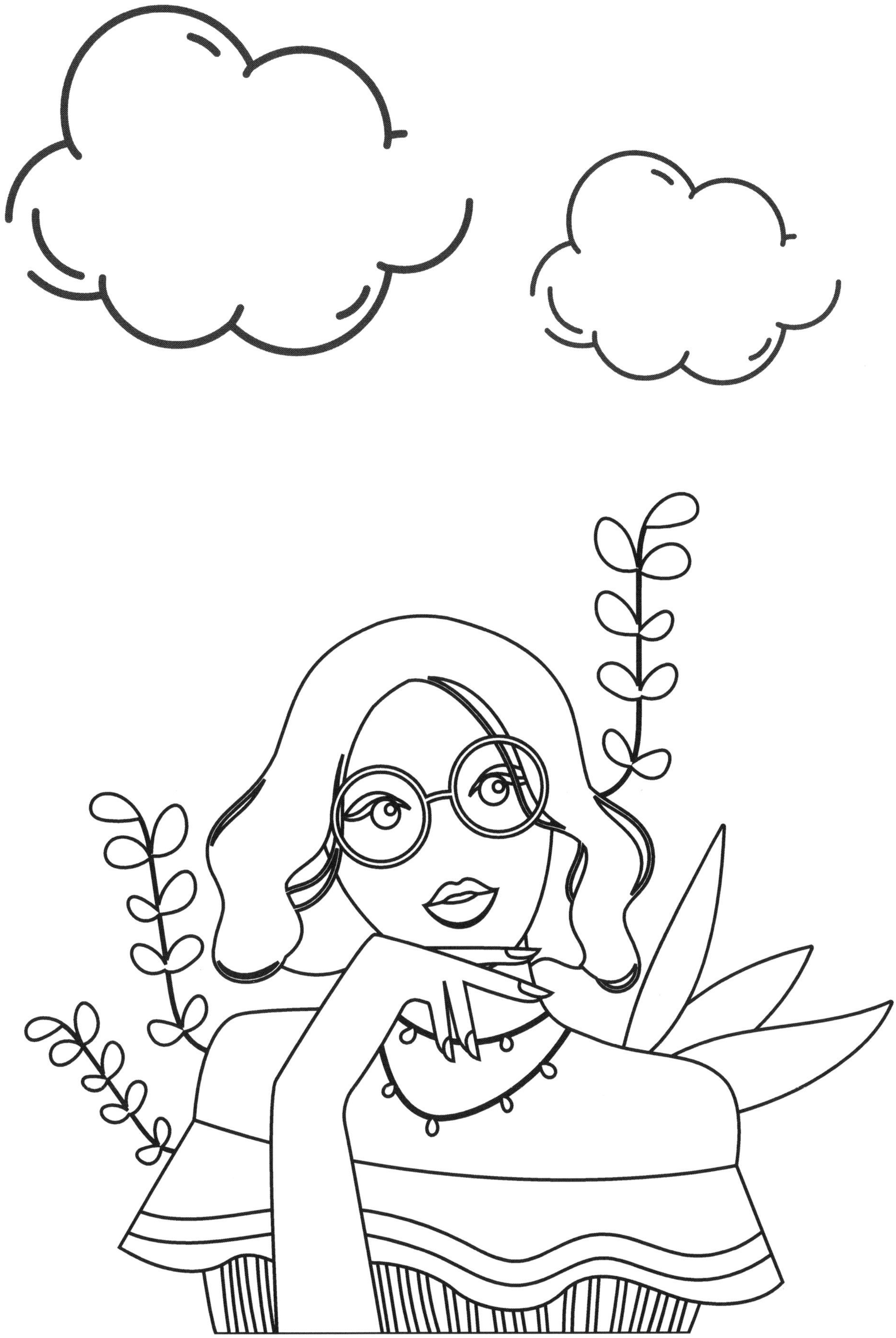

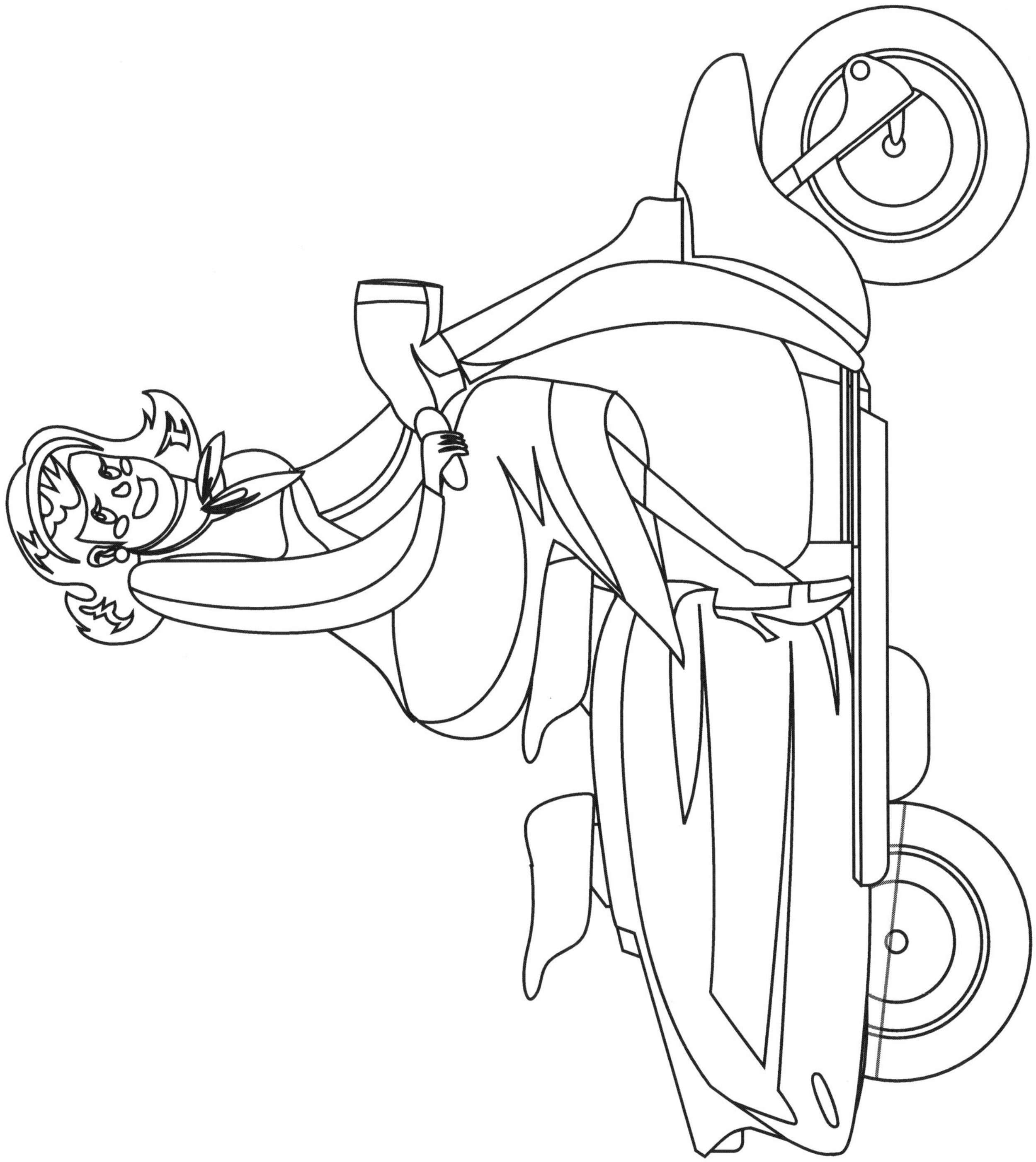

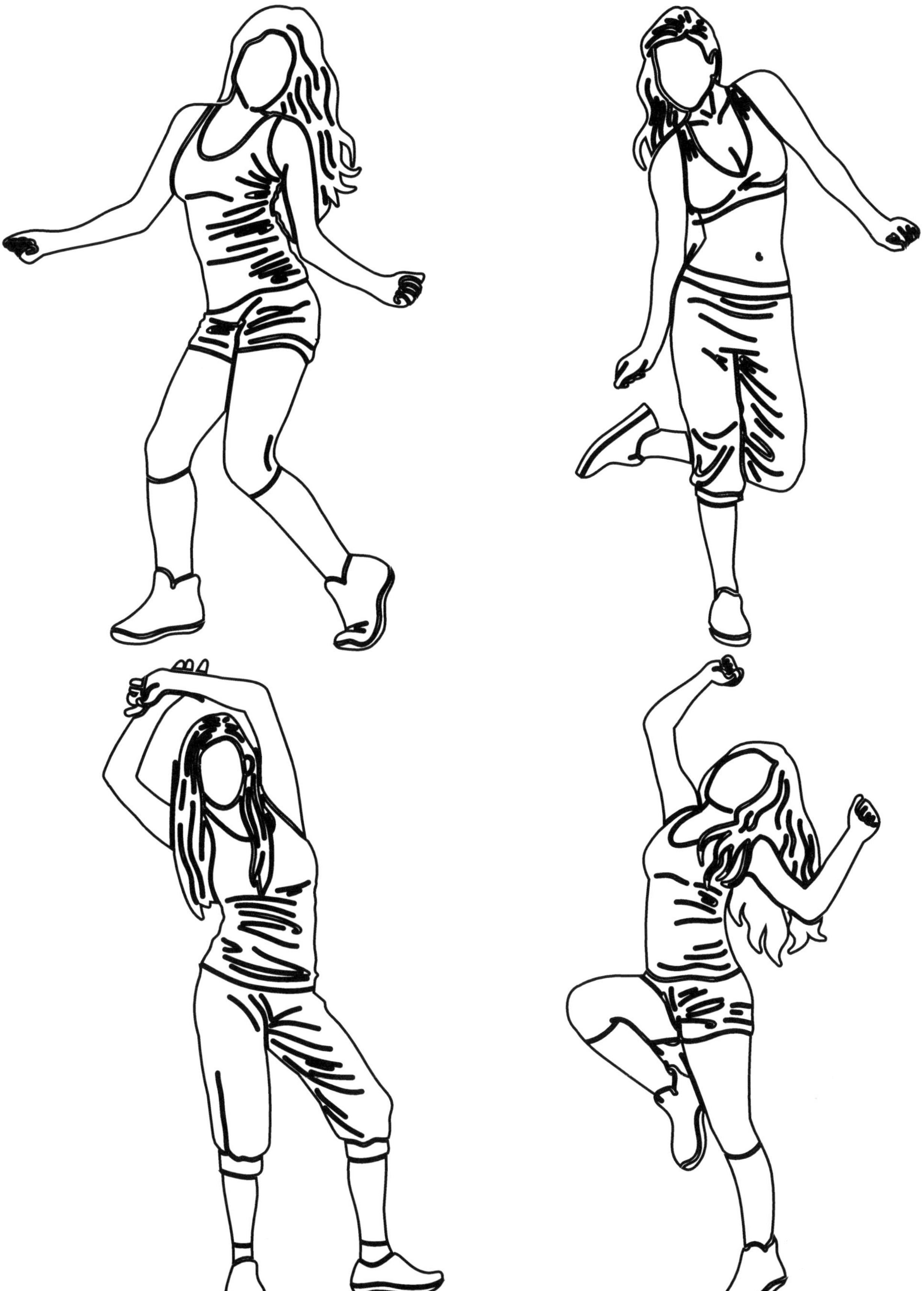

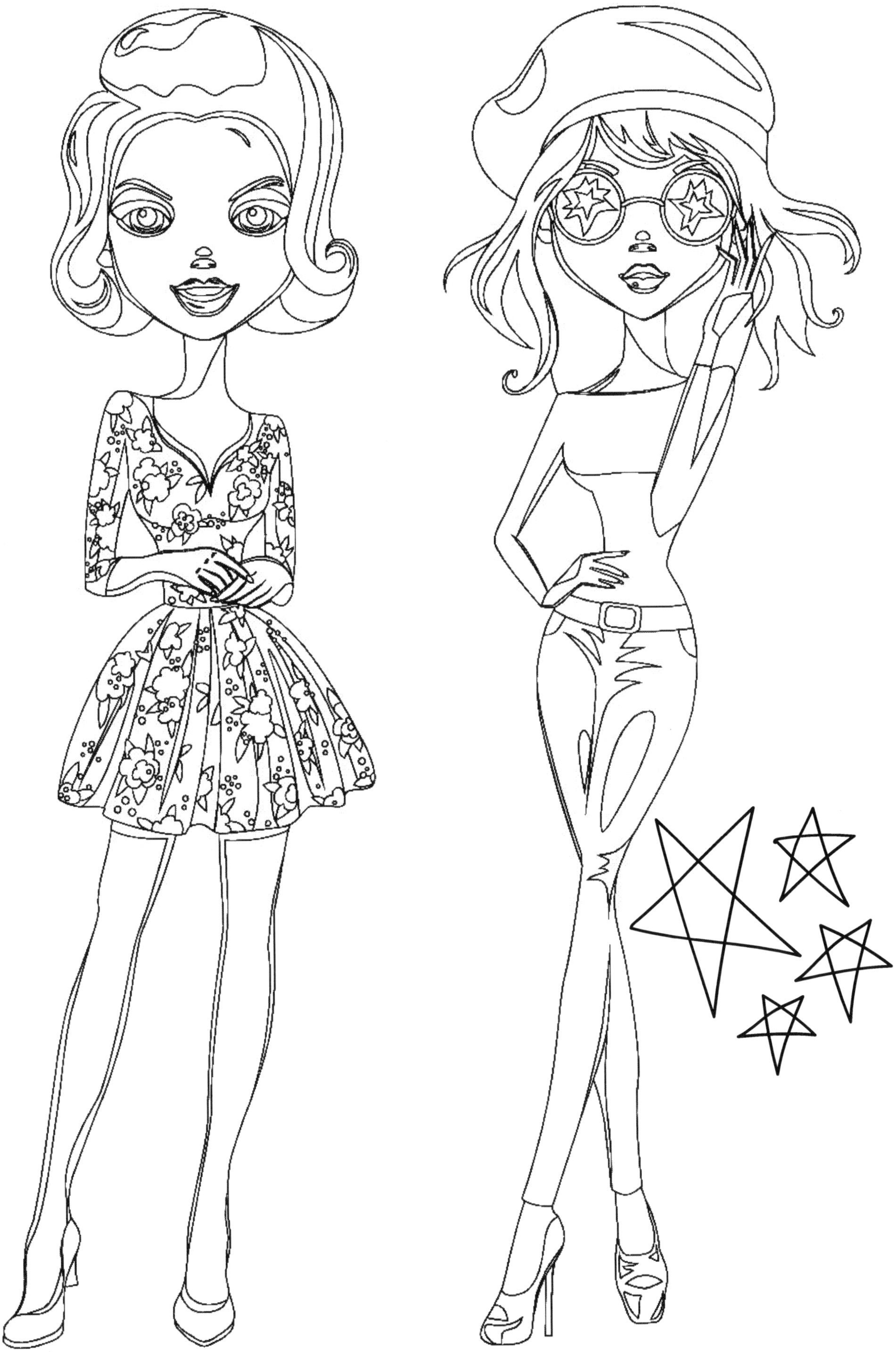

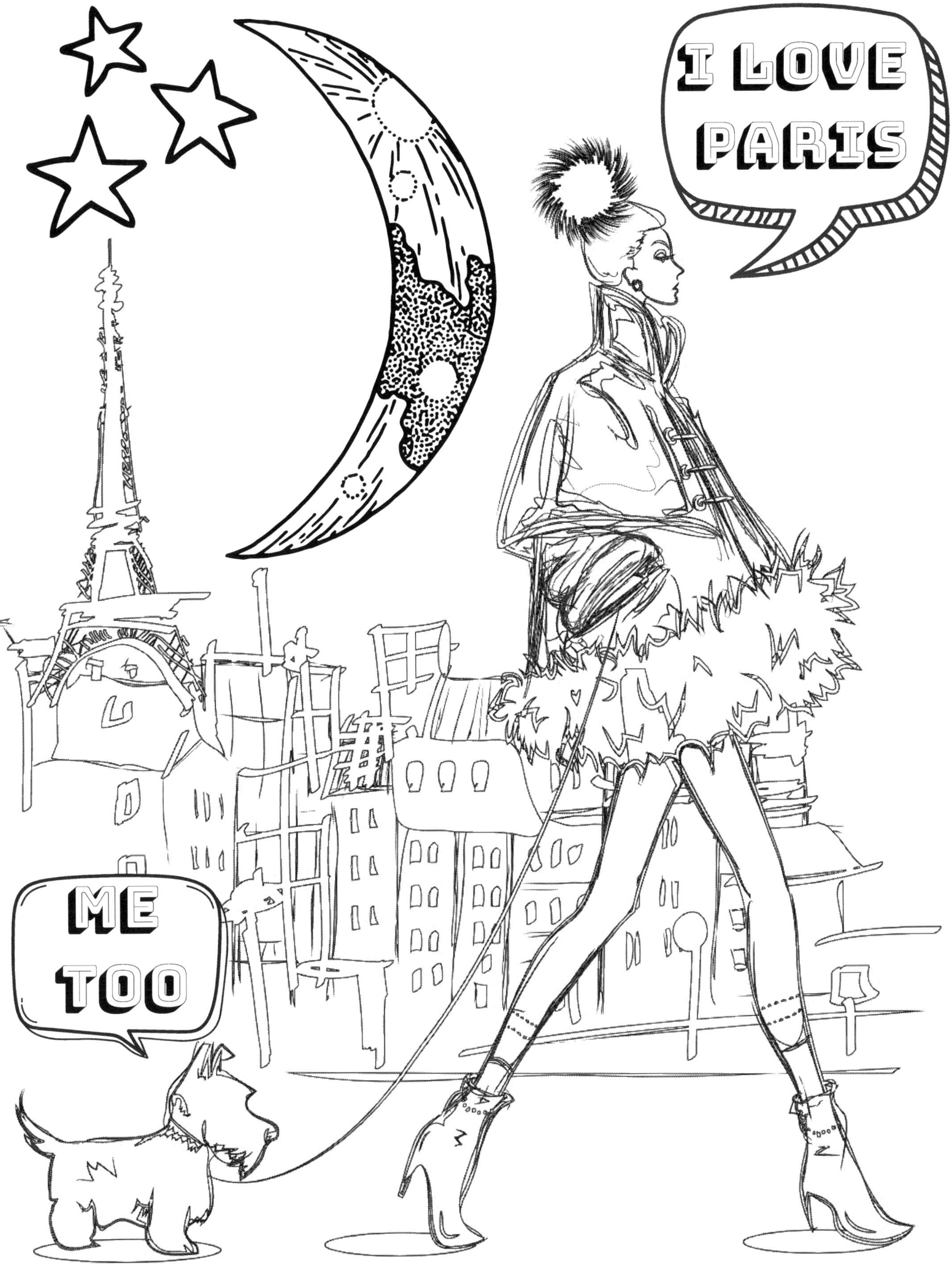
I LOVE PARIS
ME TOO

FASHION !

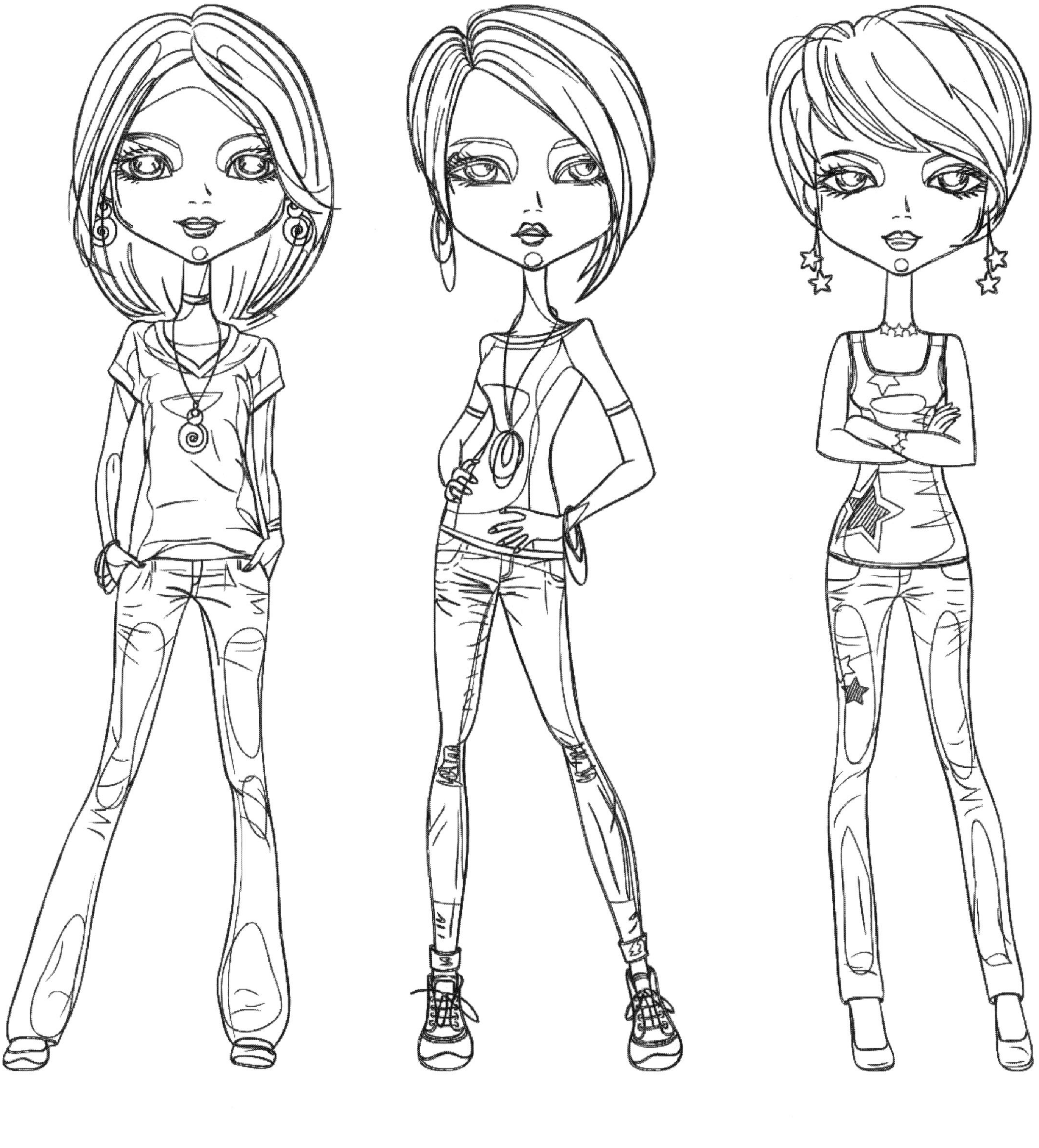

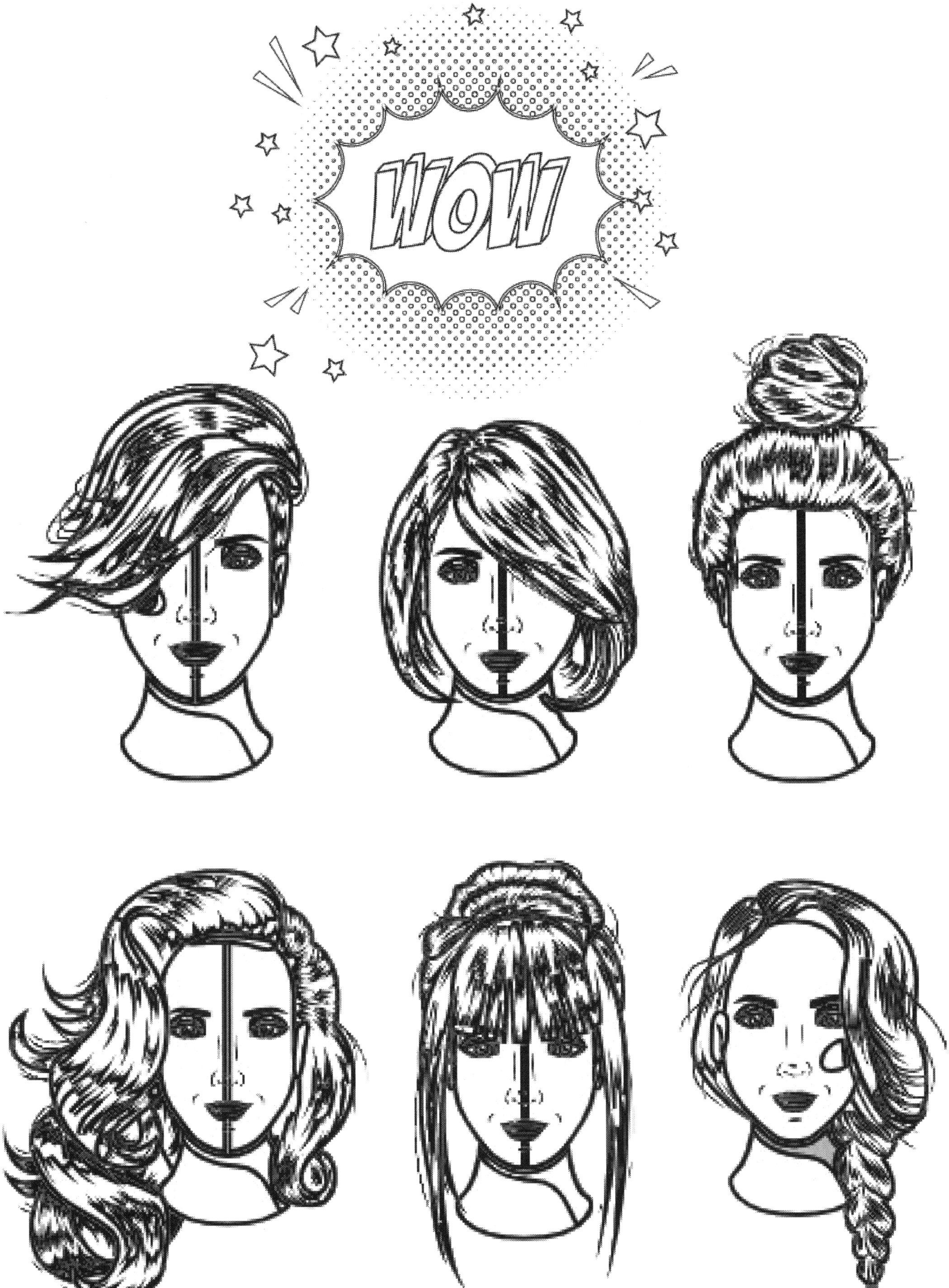
WOW

MY BAGS

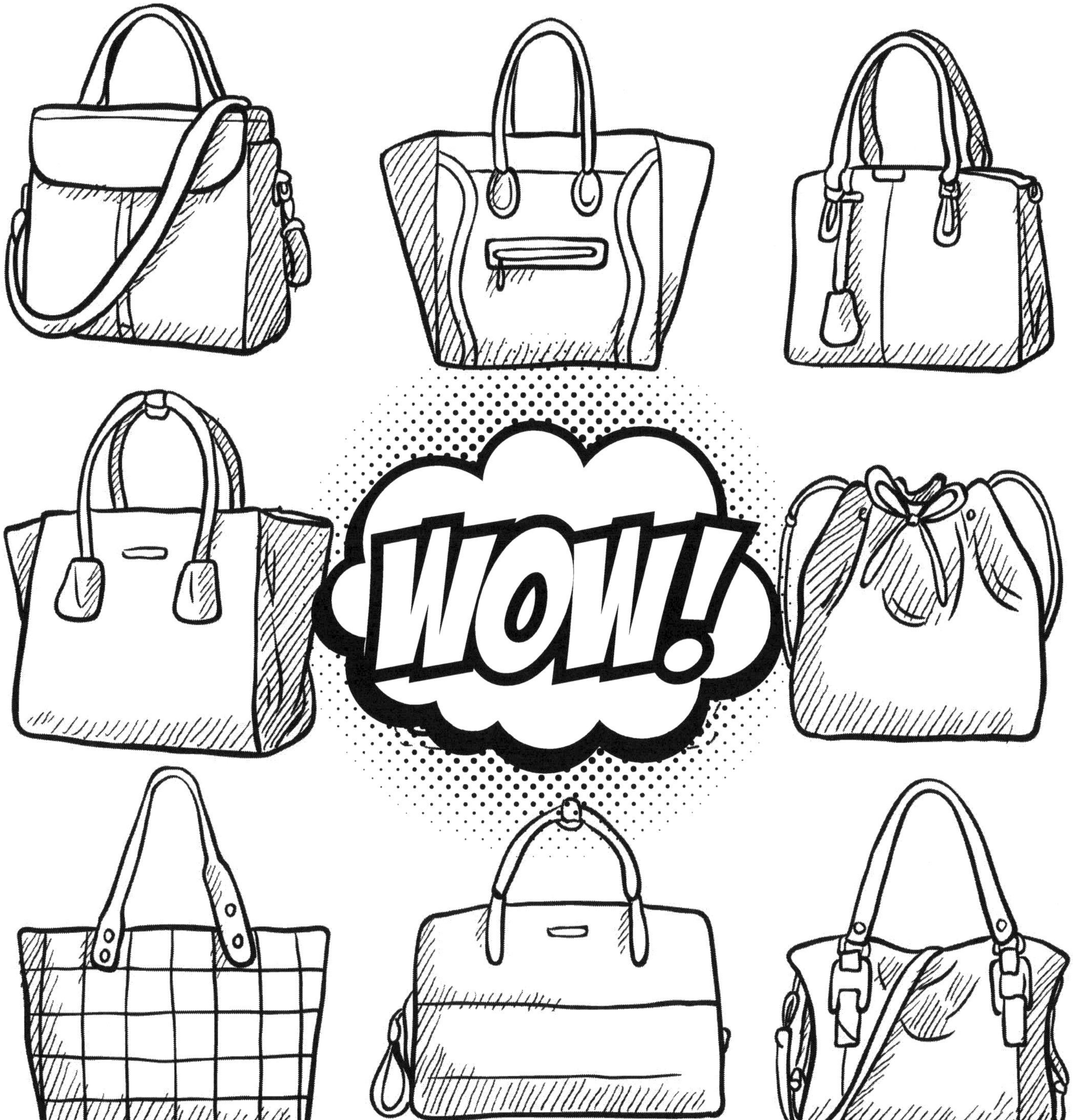

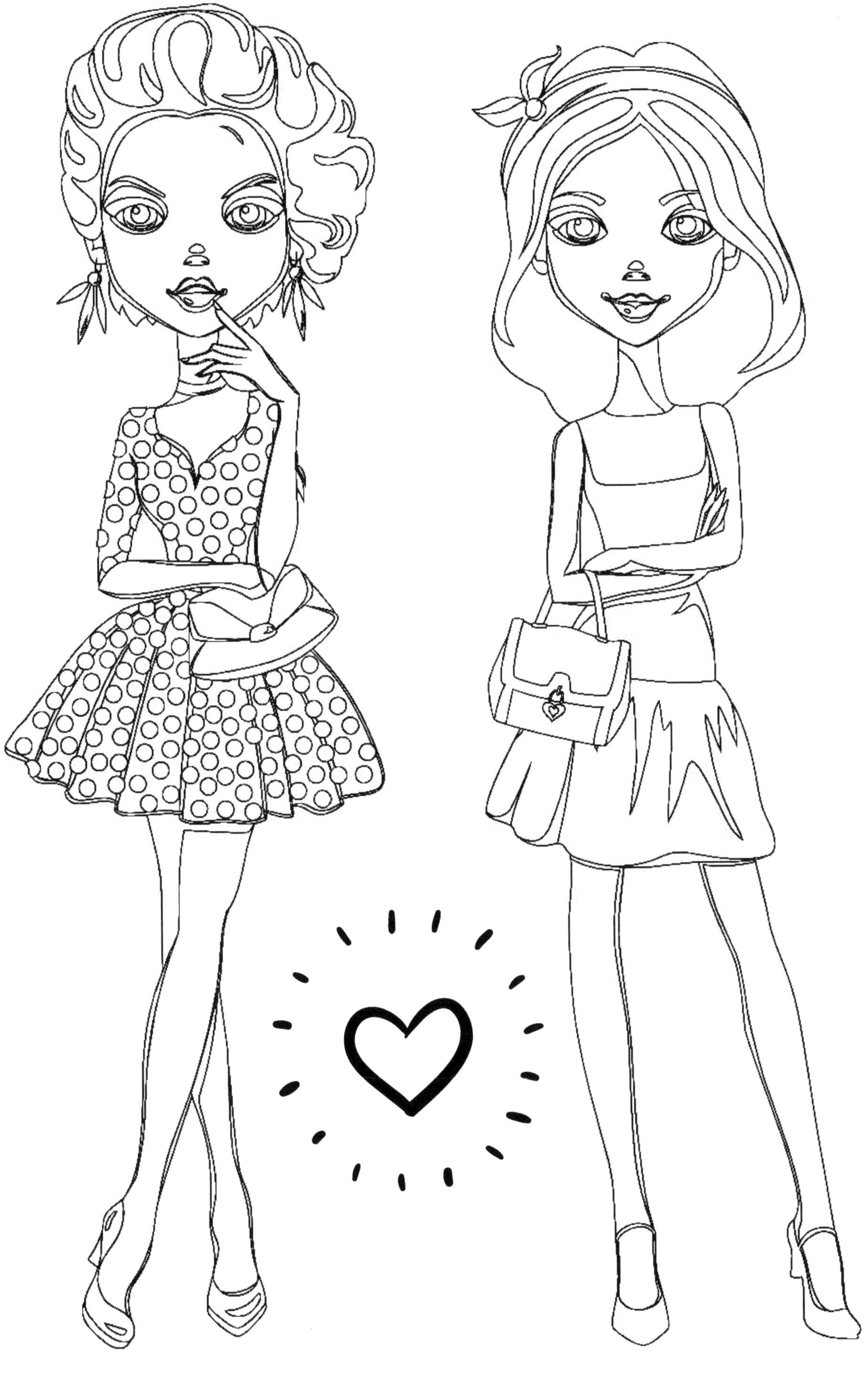

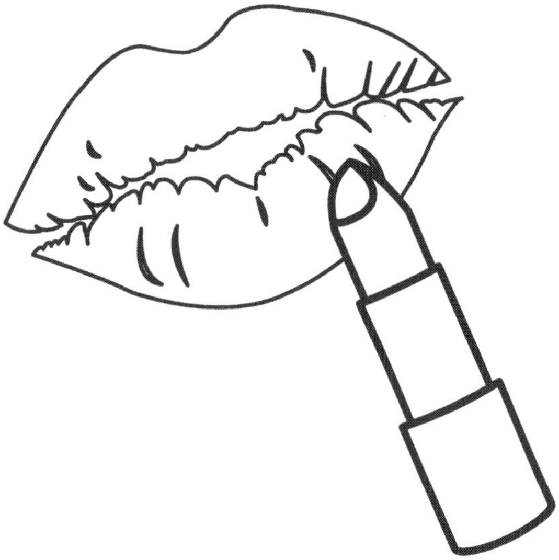

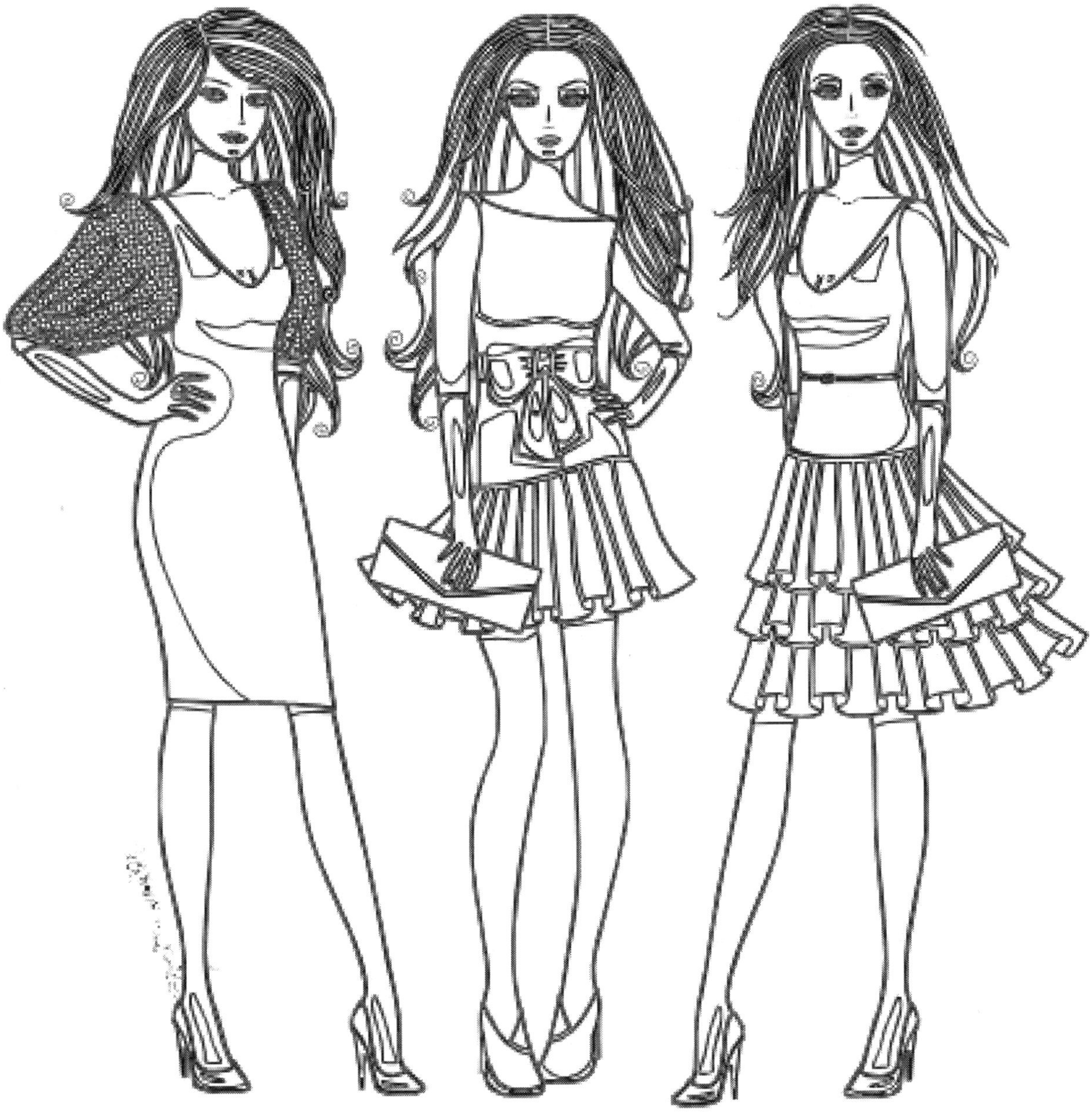

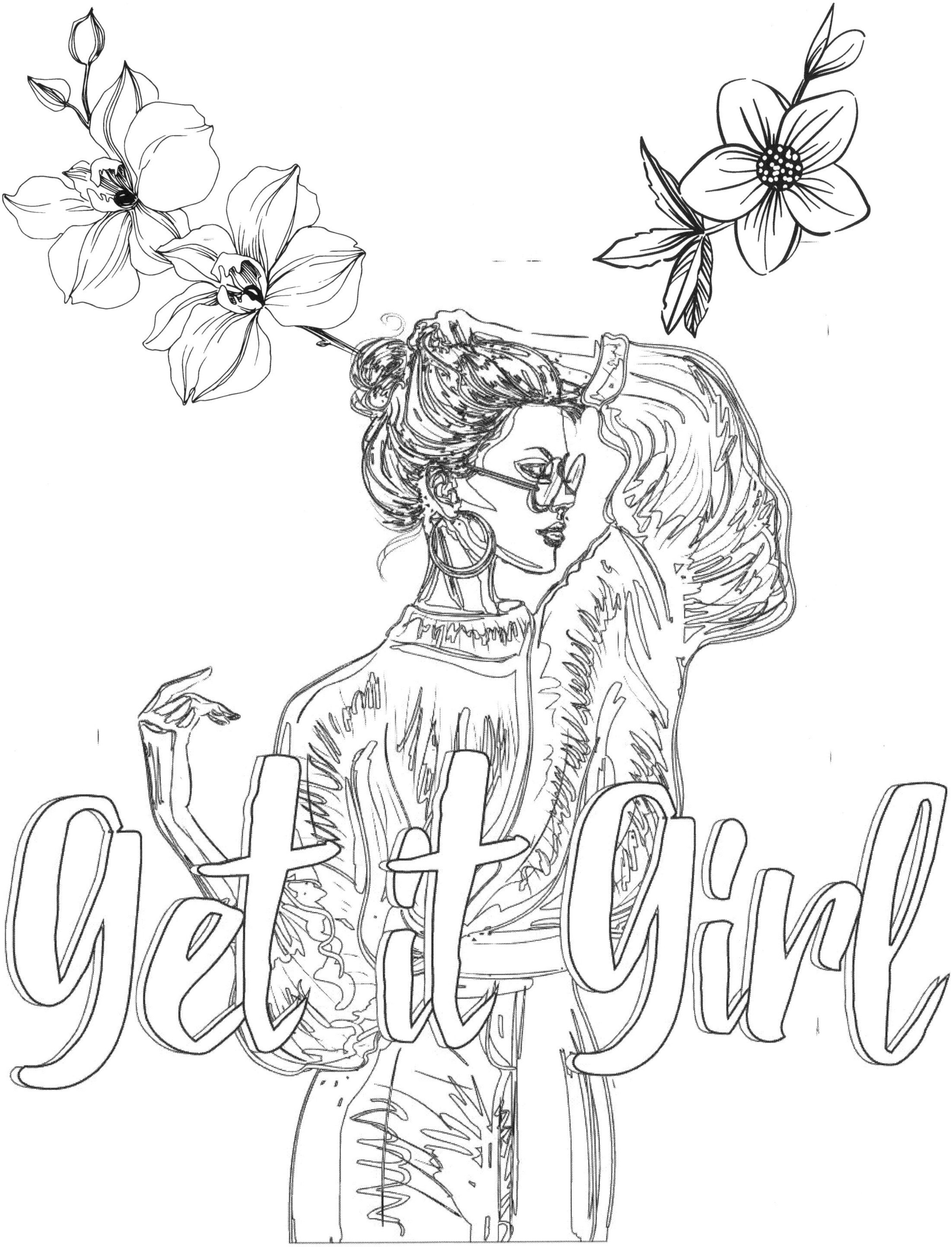
Get it Girl

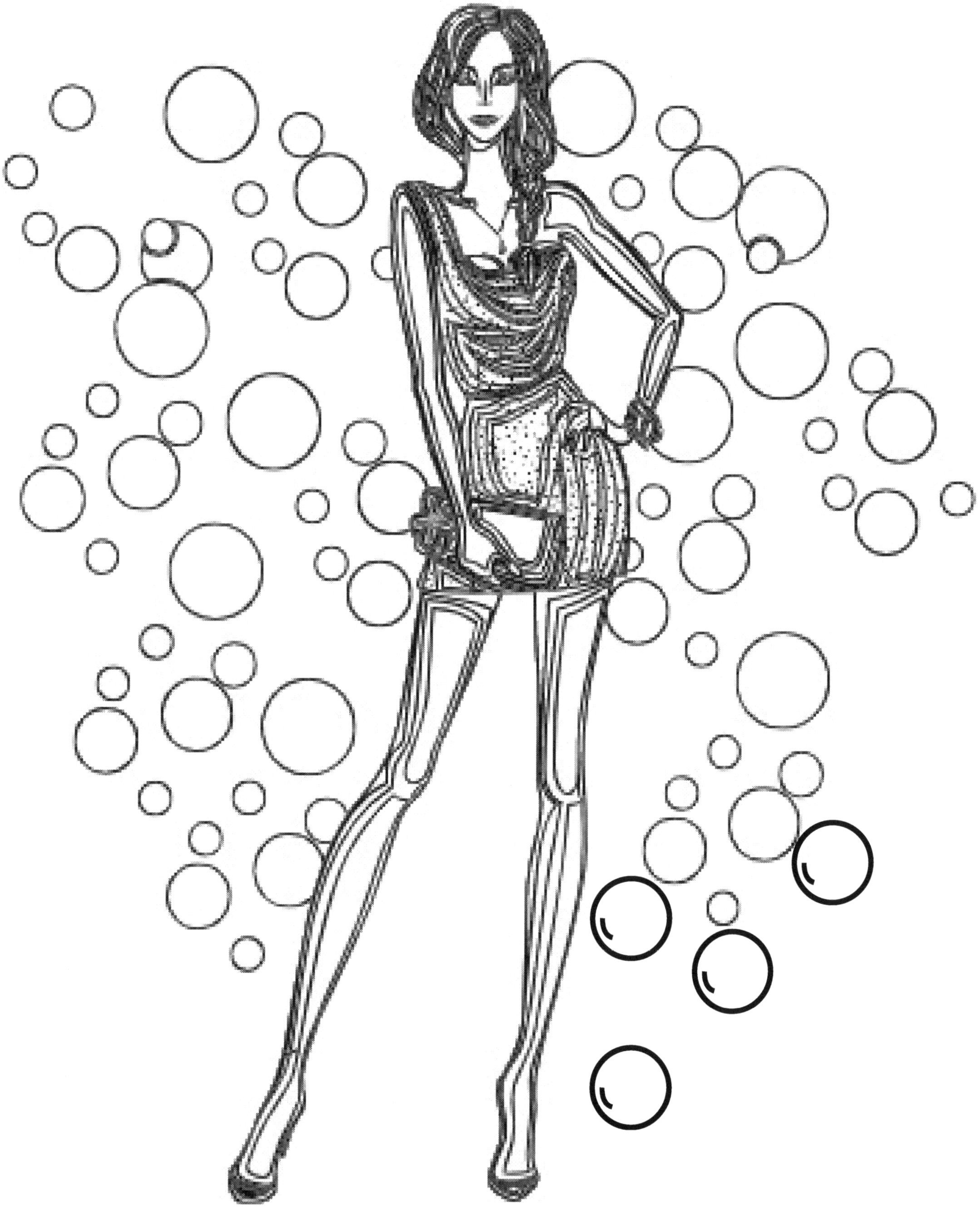

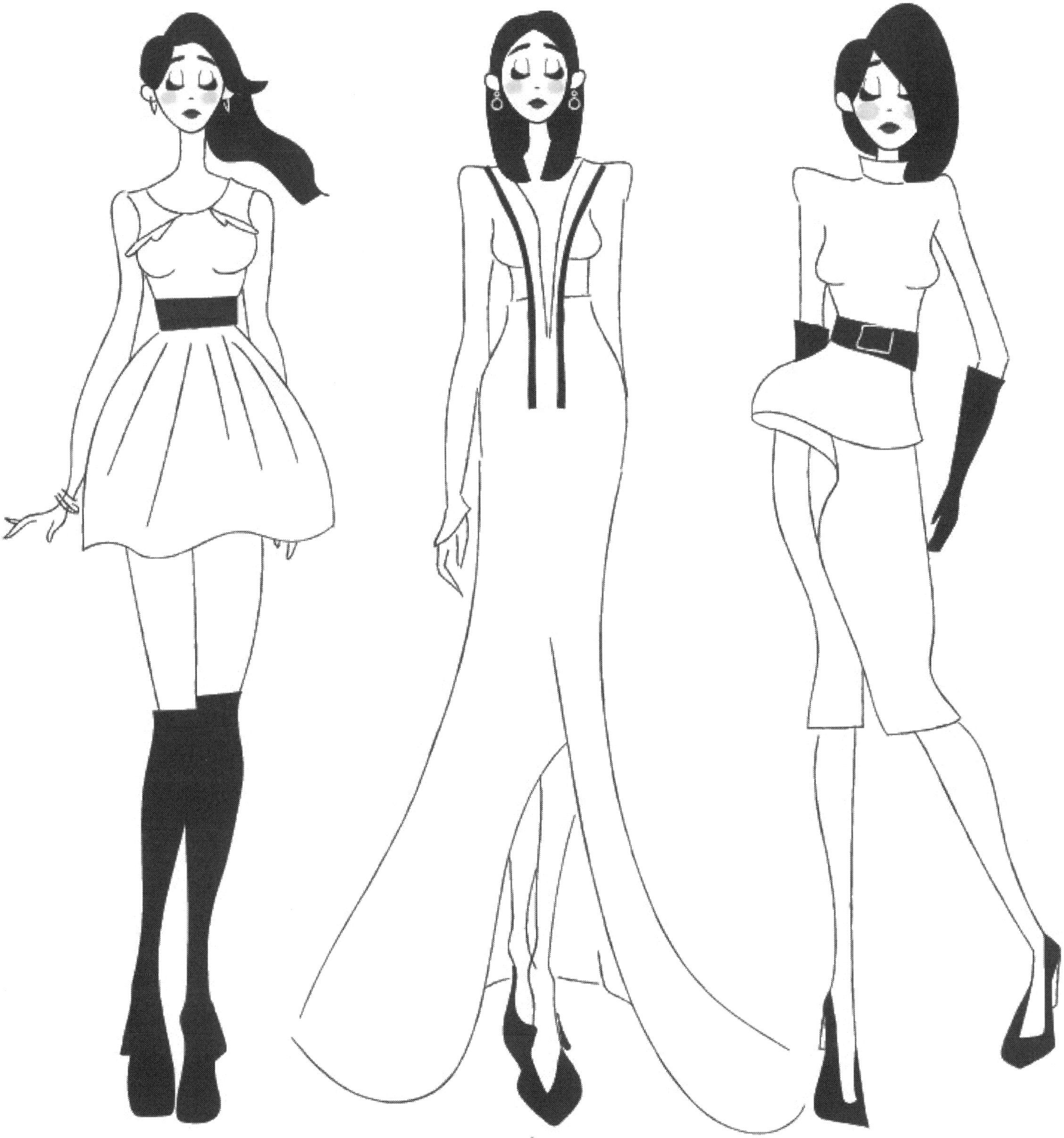

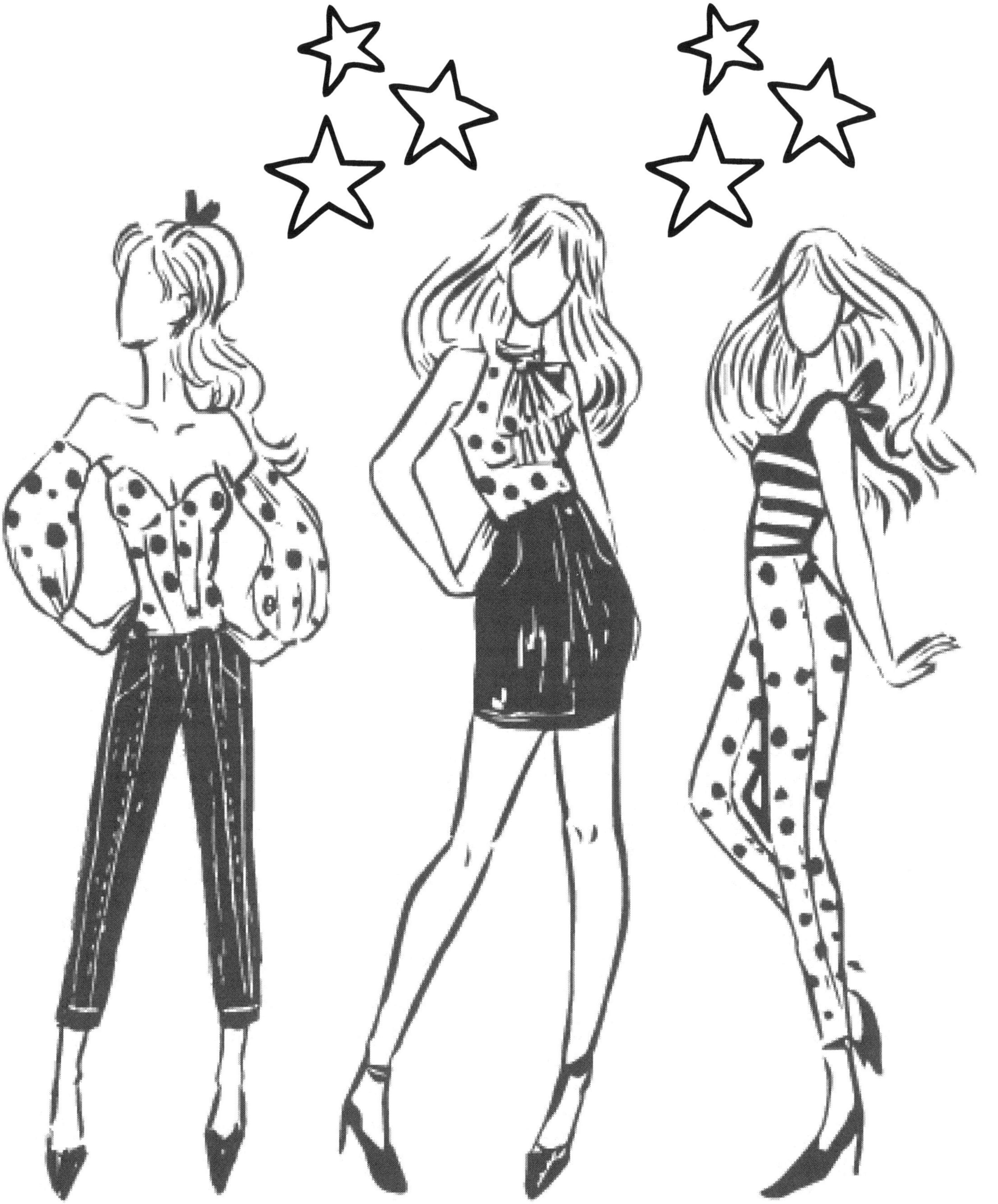

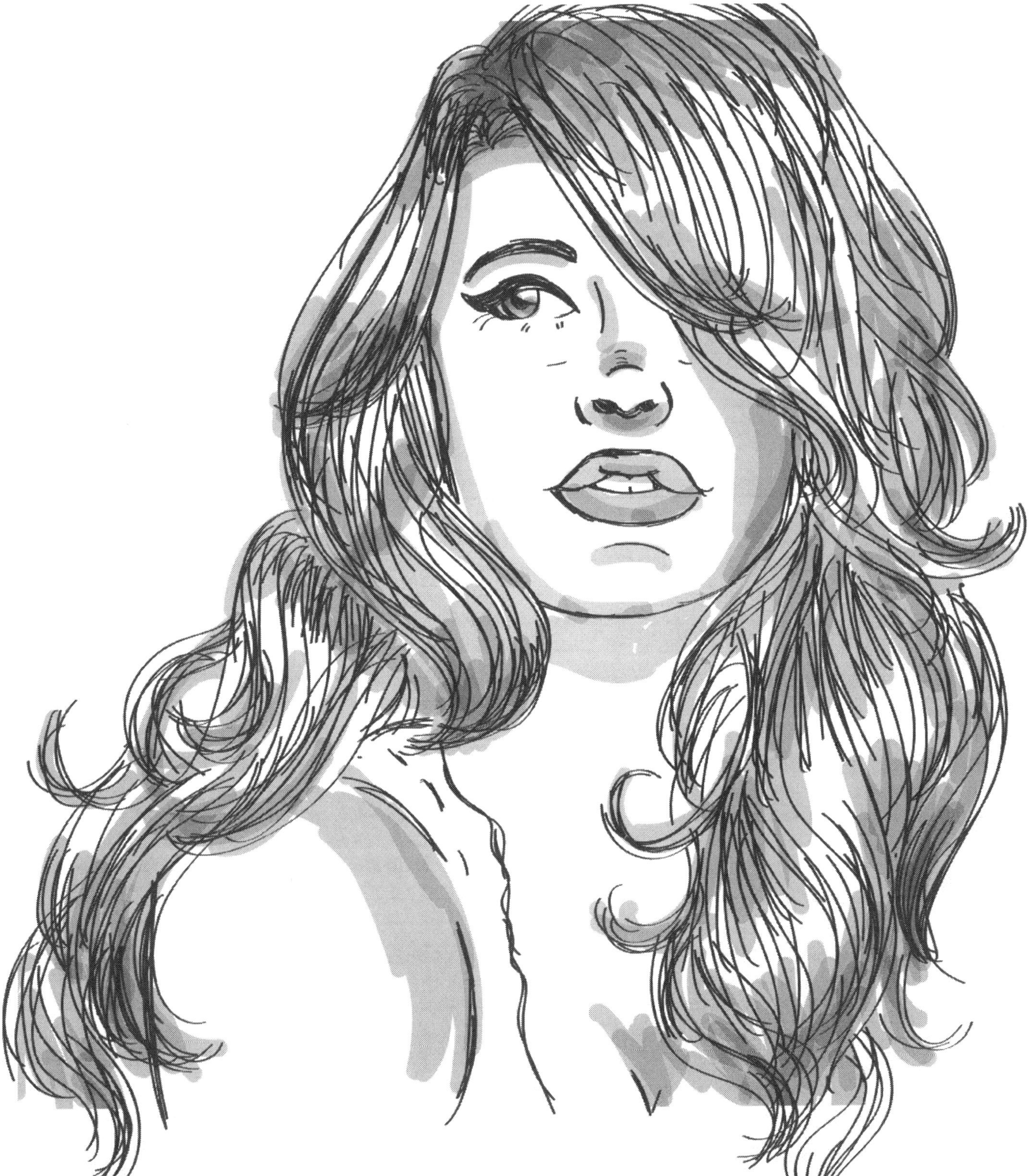

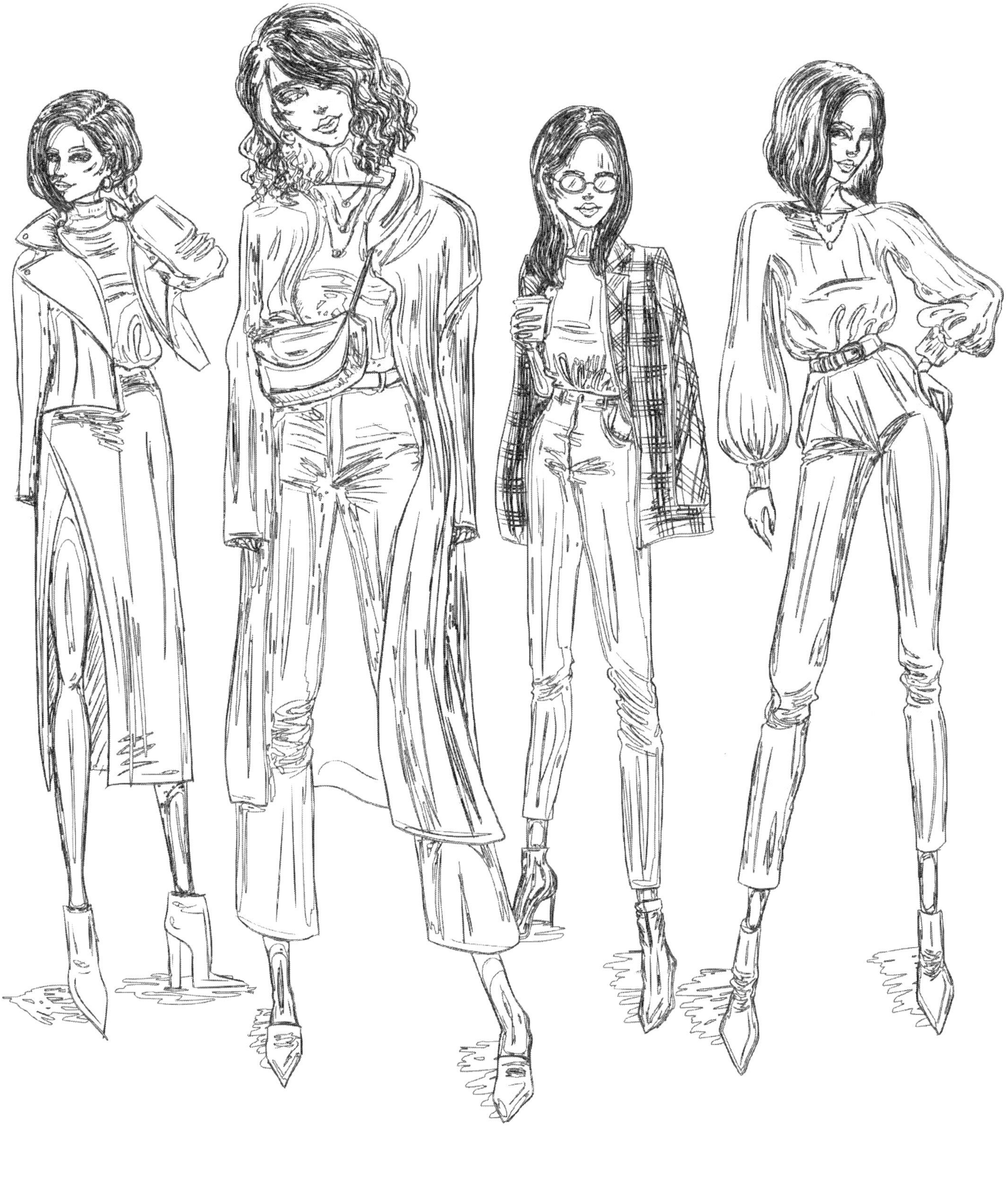

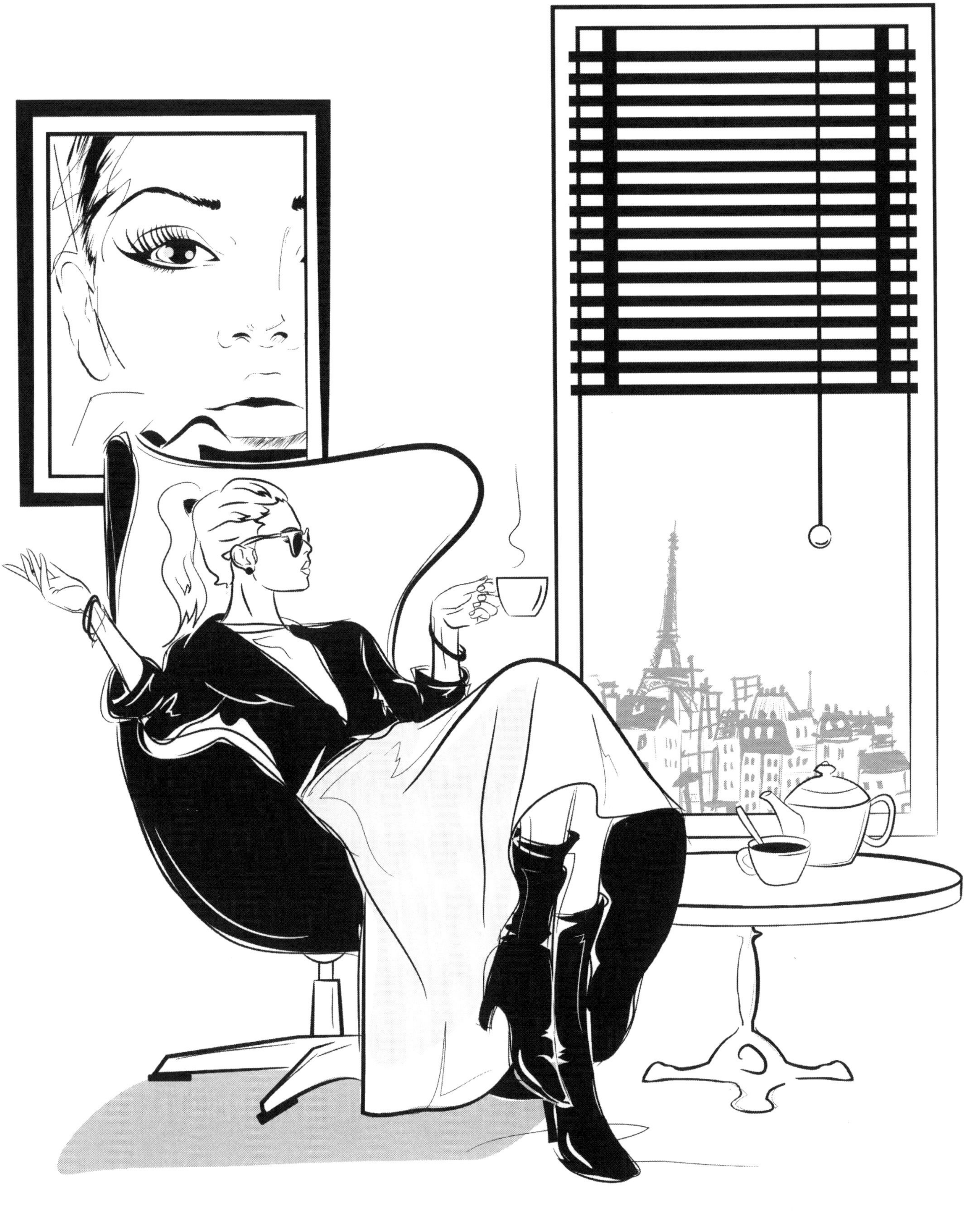